To Gina,

Saw this
of you, its
a laugh!

love Mam x.

Published in the UK by
POWERFRESH Limited
21 Rothersthorpe Crescent
Northampton
NN4 8JD

Telephone   0845 130 4565
Facsimile   0845 130 4563
E Mail   info@powerfresh.co.uk

ISBN   190292925X

Printed in Belgium by Proost N.V. International Book Production
Powerfresh September 2002

A Modern Babe's Little Book of Spells

Spells to Improve Yourself

If you feel you need a man
But don't look as good as you can
Then hold this book in your hand
And read aloud one of these chants...

These Spells come with no guarantees but we wish you lots of luck!

A Spell to Make a Bum Smaller

"Big is my bum, big are my thighs
Because I've eaten too many deep fries.
Make this Magic work really hard
To take away my excess lard.
Make me trim, make me slim
So I can give up the bloody gym."

A Spell to Repair your Virginity

"Slapper I am, Slapper I be
Sprites of youth, hear my plea.
Please repair what once I did lose
The night when I had too much booze.
Make me afresh, make me anew
Stuff up well my wanton flue."

A Spell for
the Perfect Tan

"As I am incredibly pale and white
And go beetroot red in the merest sunlight
I wish to develop the perfect tan
To attract a gorgeous hunky man.
Make my skin all bronzed and brown
So I can flash myself around town."

A Spell for Bigger Boobs

"Alakazam, Alakazear
Make my flat chest disappear.
In it's place put a large bust
With the help of this Magic Dust.
Forget double D, forget double E
Make them a whopping double G."

A Spell to Stop you Getting Older

"All the years are rushing by
And each new wrinkle makes me cry.
So I call upon the powers of youth
To help me beat the ghastly truth.
To keep me young and ever so sprightly
Raving and grooving daily and nightly."

A Spell for a Special Makeover

"Past it I am
Past it I be
Make me young and gorgeous to see.
No more wrinkles,
No more cares
No more long unwanted hairs."

A Spell to Improve Droopy Boobs

"My boobs now reach down to my belly
And feel as though they're filled with jelly.
Make them pert,
Make them alert,
No longer hanging down to my skirt."

19

A Spell to Banish PMT

"Alakazam, Alakazear
Make my PMT disappear.
No longer do I want to be
A ranting, raving, crazed banshee.
Make me lovely and full of fun
Not wanting to tout a submachine gun."

A Spell for the Perfect Body

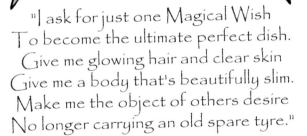

"I ask for just one Magical Wish
To become the ultimate perfect dish.
Give me glowing hair and clear skin
Give me a body that's beautifully slim.
Make me the object of others desire
No longer carrying an old spare tyre."

A Spell for Manageable Hair

"I'm sick of my hair being a bird's nest
And never being able to look my best.
So with the power of fairy magic and luck
Give me a permanent perfect look.
No more knots, no more frizz
Thanks to a magical sparkle, fizz,
bang, whizz."

A Spell to Make you a Great Dancer

"I wish for a pair of Magical feet
As I step on the dance floor to
a musical beat.
Keep me grooving like a disco diva
Moving and raving with dancing fever."

Spells to Help You Get A Man

If you still need the help of a Spell
To get a man with whom to dwell
Then hold this book in your hand
And read aloud one of these chants...

These Spells come with no guarantees but we wish you lots of luck!

A Spell to Get A Millionaire

"I wouldn't want to say I'm a
gold digging bitch
But I need a man who's incredibly rich.
So make my life magically spell bound
And create me a handsome man with
a few million pound.
Then I ask all that's magical to hear my plea
And make him fall in love with me."

Three Wishes
for a Single Girl

"I call upon the Fairy Folk
To use their wands in one Magic stroke.
To this Gorgeous Girl they'll grant
Three wishes to use and enchant.
I wish for money, I wish for joy,
I wish for a handsome fit Toy Boy."

A Spell to Get a Boyfriend

To meet a man who's right for you
Whom you hope is fun and easy to woo.
Hold this book tight in your hand
And read aloud this Magical Chant.

" I need some love and lots of attention
Some T.L.C. and need I mention
Lots of fun both night and day
And someone to cherish in every way."

A Spell for
Everlasting Love

"I'd like a life that's really great
To share with the perfect mate.
So make me a love that grows and grows
Like a seed that you sow.
Make it last forever and ever
Getting better whatsoever."

A Spell to Make you Irresistible

"With this Mystic Spell I wish
To become a gorgeous irresistible dish.
Making everyone I meet
Fall in reverence at my feet.
Give me a well toned body to flex
So I can pull the opposite sex."

A Spell for Everlasting Happiness

"May the powers of happiness and joy
Fill my life with lots to enjoy.
Make me and mine forever happy
Never rowing or getting too snappy.
Make everyday full of sun
Falling on me and everyone."

A Spell for the Perfect Kiss

"As I've kissed many a frog
And found no Prince worth a snog
Find me a man who is gorgeous and fit
Who's up for a snog and a bit of crumpet.
Make it moist,
Make it long
And make him wear a tiny thong."

A Spell to Improve your Sex Life

"My sex life is now very sad
And goes from dull to extremely bad.
So I call on the powers of debauchery
To make my life more of an orgy.
I'd like to swing from the chandelier
And use with style my God-given gear."

A Spell for the Perfect Man

"Now I'm after a new man in my life
So I can become someone's wife
I wish for a man who's hunky and cute
Not some old fashioned
Neanderthal brute.
Make him classy, make him romantic
But most of all make his willy gigantic."

A Spell to Get an Engagement Ring

"As I've found the man for me
I need him to get down on bended knee
So I wish for roses and a bottle of wine
With a romantic proposal as we dine.
Then make my new ring shine so bright
That people think it's a new source of light."

49

A Spell for a Special Wedding Day

"We call upon the Wedding Dove
To make our lives full of love.
Make us lucky, make us happy.
Help us to never get too snappy.
Ensure we last for evermore
Through good and bad and love and war.
Make every day feel brand new
And keep the sex fantastic too."

Spells to Change a Man

(Because they always go downhill)

If your man is no longer as perfect
as the day you met
And you really are starting to fret
Then hold this book in your hand
And read aloud one of these chants...

These Spells come with no guarantees but we wish you lots of luck!

A Spell to Cure Baldness

"Slaphead he is, Slaphead he be
Totally bald for the World to see.
No more wigs shall he need
Once his head begins to seed.
So give him locks of wonderful hair
That give him panache and savoir faire."

A Spell to Get
Rid of
Bad Breath

"I hate the smell of booze and cigs
That come from the mouth of
my slovenly pig.
I wish to improve this terrible smell
And escape my life of stinky hell.
So make my man smell really sweet
So our next snog is a complete treat."

A Spell to Reduce a Beer Belly

"My bloke's belly has been stretched
by gallons of beer
And he's appeared pregnant for years and years.
So I call upon this Magic Power
To fall upon him in a shining shower.
To take away his excess weight
So he no longer looks like a shipping crate.
Make him slim, make him thin
So he can see where his feet begin."

A Spell to Cure a Lager Lout

"I'm sick of the constant
'Boys' Nights Out'
When he arrives home a drunken lager lout.
So with the Magic in this Spell
Make my life less like hell.
Make me, again, the 'apple of his eye'
As he wines and dines me from morning
till nigh'."

A Spell for a Football Addict

"My man is driving me insane
With his love of the football game.
So with the Magic in this rhyme
Make it forever full time.
Make my tele footie free
So he pays more attention to me."

A Spell to Improve a Man's Toilet Habits

"I'm sick of the seat never being down
Or puddles of urine that make me frown.
I wish for a bathroom that's always
spick and span
Without the odour of a smelly pan.
So make my fella always think twice
And make his aim more precise."

A Spell to Cure Bad Wind

"My bloke's bottom is rather breezy
And makes our friends feel
somewhat queasy.
His bum is emitting an odious smell
Which needs sorting with this spell.
Please make it so that his insides
Smell less like something crawled
up there and died."

A Spell to Make
a Willy Bigger

"My man's life is dogged by a lack of girth
Making him a figure of mirth.
No longer shall he feel so silly
For carrying around his little willy
Once I have said this Magical Chant
A Canoe you'll find inside his pants."

A Spell for a TV Slob

"My man never moves from our sofa
As he's a complete TV loafer.
So with this Magic shift his ass
Before he becomes an ugly fat mass.
Make him active, make him fit
No longer a 'remote control-hogging git'."

A Spell to Get
Rid of Excess
Body Hair

"Now my man's sprouting hair
In his nose, ears and everywhere
I wish for a spell to take them away
Before they go long curly and grey.
Make him as smooth as a new born baby
Not like a man of over eighty."

A Spell to Cure Smelly Feet

"My man's feet really stink
And I worry what other people think.
So with the power of this Magical Spell
Help him get rid of the cheesy smell.
No more Cheddar,
No more Cheshire,
Instead a scent to really treasure."

A Spell to
Make a Man Fitter

My man has now let himself go
Allowing his body to grow and grow.
So using the magic in fairy spit
Make him awake amazingly fit
With massive pecs, a muscly back
And the sexiest looking six-pack."

Spells to Dump a Man

(If all else fails)

If it is time to get rid of your man
And you've done all you can
Then hold this book in your hand
And read aloud one of these chants...

These Spells come with no guarantees but we wish you lots of luck!

A Dear John Spell

"As I am useless at dumping men
I thought I'd write him with my pen
But as I can't think of what to say
I ask this spell to guide my way.
I want to tell him that we're through
So I can find someone exciting and new."

A Spell to Swap a Bloke

"I want to trade in my guy
And give a new one a three month try.
So swap my lazy old man
For one with muscles and a tan.
Make him hunky, make him cute
And make him have loads of loot."

A Spell to Get Over a Cheating Husband

"My man's found someone new in his life
But as I am still his wedded wife
I need some help from this Magic power
To help me now I'm bitter and sour.
So I wish to get over him
With the help of a gorgeous hunk from the gym."

A Spell to Let a Bloke Down Gently

"This guy I've met is kind of 'nice'
But doesn't possess any kind of spice
In fact I'd say he's rather dull
Not gorgeous or cute or masterful.
But I wish to let him down slow
And not hurt his 'nice' tender ego.
So all that's Magic hear my plea
And let him forget he ever met me."

A Spell for a Useless Bloke

"As my man is now no good
And has become a piece of dead wood
I wish to make more use of him
Using this Magic here within.
So turn him into a new dishwasher
Instead of an idle lazy to**er."

A Spell to Stop a Guy Calling

"My phone is forever ringing off the hook
Because of a guy who's completely mistook
He thinks I'm interested in his body
And wants me to be his bit of totty.
So with the Magic in this spell
Make him understand the words
'Go to Hell'."

A Spell to Turn a Man into a Toad

"My man treats me really bad
And is an absolute sexist cad.
In order to get my own back
I'd like to turn him into a Natter-Jack.
So I call upon the Magic in this rhyme
To turn him into a toad, the rotten swine."

A Spell for Revenge on a Love Rat

"I've discovered my man has cheated on me
So all that's Magic hear my plea.
Make his willy only rise
When he's around other guys
So all his days are filled with fear
As he starts to wonder if he's turned queer."

A Spell to Dump a Bloke

"As I'm sick of my present bloke
Because he's turned into a bit of a joke
With the help of the Magic here
I wish to make him disappear.
No creeping phone call, no written
'Dear John'
Just a fella who is suddenly gone."

A Spell for a Quick and Easy Divorce

" Now my marriage is completely through
To the partner I thought I knew
Make our divorce quick and easy
Without it getting overly sleazy.
Ensure I get the money and house
Once I'm rid of my lousy spouse."